The 1970s
Decade in Photos
Protest and Change

Jim Corrigan

Enslow Publishers, Inc.
40 Industrial Road
Box 398
Berkeley Heights, NJ 07922
USA

http://www.enslow.com

Library of Congress Cataloging-in-Publication Data

Corrigan, Jim.
  The 1970s decade in photos : protest and change / by Jim Corrigan.
     p. cm. — (Amazing decades in photos)
  Includes bibliographical references and index.
  Summary: "Middle school readers will find out about the important world, national, and cultural developments of the decade 1970-1979"—Provided by publisher.
  ISBN-13: 978-0-7660-3136-4
  ISBN-10: 0-7660-3136-5
  1. United States—History—1969—Pictorial works—Juvenile literature. 2. History, Modern—20th century—Pictorial works—Juvenile literature. 3. Nineteen seventies—Pictorial works—Juvenile literature. I. Title. II. Title: Nineteen seventies decade in photos.
  E855.C685 2009
  973.924—dc22

                                                                                     2008042998

Printed in the United States of America.

092009 Lake Book Manufacturing, Inc., Melrose Park, IL

10 9 8 7 6 5 4 3 2 1

To Our Readers: We have done our best to make sure all Internet Addresses in this book were active and appropriate when we went to press. However, the author and the publisher have no control over and assume no liability for the material available on those Internet sites or on other Web sites they may link to. Any comments or suggestions can be sent by email to comments@enslow.com or to the address on the back cover.

Every effort has been made to locate all copyright holders of material used in this book. If any errors or omissions have occurred, corrections will be made in future editions of this book.

♻ Enslow Publishers, Inc., is committed to printing our books on recycled paper. The paper in every book contains 10% to 30% post-consumer waste (PCW). The cover board on the outside of each book contains 100% PCW. Our goal is to do our part to help young people and the environment too!

Produced by OTTN Publishing, Stockton, N.J.

TABLE OF CONTENTS

An American soldier wades through a river in Vietnam, 1970. The United States had become drawn into the fighting between North and South Vietnam during the 1950s. By the early 1970s, most Americans had turned against the war, and U.S. leaders were searching for a way to withdraw from Vietnam.

WELCOME TO THE 1970s

T he 1970s were a time of struggle and doubt. For three decades, America had been a world leader. Its economy thrived. Its military was strong. The nation felt confident. By the 1970s, Americans began to sense a change. Suddenly, they faced many problems. They began to wonder if their country was losing its strength. President Jimmy Carter called it a "crisis of confidence."

The Vietnam War played a large role in the crisis. American soldiers first began fighting in Vietnam during the 1960s.

The war was different from past conflicts. U.S. troops found it hard to tell friend from foe. The enemy struck quickly and then vanished. As the death toll grew, many people at home began to oppose the war. They staged protests, some of which led to bloodshed. College students were among the most vocal war protesters.

A large banner hangs over a crowd celebrating the first "Earth Day" in New York on April 22, 1970. Earth Day is an annual event held to raise awareness of environmental issues.

During the 1970s, women demonstrated to gain equal status with men in the workplace. Many women supported the proposed Equal Rights Amendment to the U.S. Constitution. This would have made it illegal to discriminate against someone based on gender. However, the amendment was not ratified by enough states to become part of federal law.

Another conflict in the world caused many problems during the 1970s. It was the Arab-Israeli conflict. In 1948, Jewish people created the state of Israel in the Middle East. Arab nations there strongly opposed Israel. They fought several wars to destroy it, but failed. Some Arab groups turned to terrorism. They hijacked airplanes. In 1972, they took hostages at the Olympics.

America's support for Israel angered the Arab countries. In 1973, Arab countries decided to stop selling oil to the United States. The move triggered a U.S. energy crisis. People ran short of gas for their cars and heating oil for their homes. America's economy was hit hard. Prices for food and other goods climbed. The government urged everyone to save fuel. The energy crisis was a major news story.

The Watergate scandal also made headlines. It involved President Richard M. Nixon and his top aides. They were caught committing illegal acts. Watergate ended Nixon's political career. He became the only president ever to resign from office. The scandal outraged many Americans. Like the Vietnam War, Watergate caused many people to distrust their government.

The 1970s saw some uplifting events as well. An American swimmer named Mark Spitz made Olympic history. Slugger Hank Aaron broke baseball's long-standing record for career home runs. In 1976, America celebrated two hundred years of independence.

However, more bad news would follow this celebration. In Jonestown, Guyana, more than nine hundred members of a religious cult took their own lives. An accident at a nuclear power plant in Pennsylvania nearly led to disaster. Such stories added to the sense of gloom many people felt during the 1970s.

As the decade ended, America seemed to reach a new low. Another energy crisis gripped the economy. In Iran, U.S. embassy workers were being held hostage. The Soviet Union—America's Cold War rival—invaded Afghanistan. Nobody knew how these crises might end. But feelings of doubt ran stronger than ever.

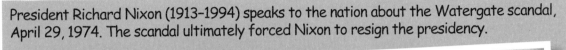

President Richard Nixon (1913–1994) speaks to the nation about the Watergate scandal, April 29, 1974. The scandal ultimately forced Nixon to resign the presidency.

WAR PROTEST TURNS DEADLY

By 1970, protests against the Vietnam War were common. Sometimes, protesters and the police fought. In May 1970, a clash at Kent State University in Ohio left four students dead.

Like most colleges, Kent State was a hub of antiwar feelings. Many students wanted an end to the Vietnam War. In 1970, President Richard M. Nixon sent U.S. troops into Cambodia, one of Vietnam's neighbors. Nixon said enemy soldiers were hiding in the jungles there. Some Americans became very angry. It seemed to them that the war was growing, not ending. On May 1, 1970, there was a riot in the city of Kent. The mayor of Kent requested that the Ohio National Guard be sent to his city to prevent further disturbances.

National Guardsmen are citizen soldiers. Most of the time, they live as civilians. They serve as soldiers during emergencies.

President Nixon points out North Vietnamese Army camps along the Cambodian border, April 30, 1970. Nixon's announcement that he would send U.S. troops into Cambodia led to antiwar protests at many American colleges.

Students at Kent State University take part in a protest against U.S. involvement in the Vietnam War. On May 1, 1970, about five hundred students demonstrated on the campus. The protest was meant to be peaceful. However, that night police had to put down a violent disturbance in a town near the campus.

On May 2, about a thousand Ohio National Guardsmen arrived in Kent. Most took up positions on Kent State University's campus. Around noon on May 4, approximately one hundred National Guardsmen faced a large crowd of student protesters on the campus. The students were ordered to leave. Some of the students hurled rocks. Finally, some of the Guardsmen fired their rifles into the crowd. Four students were killed. Nine more were wounded.

Just ten days later, a similar incident took place in Mississippi. Police shot and killed two students at Jackson State College. The killings at Kent State and Jackson State shocked many Americans and spurred further protests across the nation.

Members of the Ohio National Guard launch tear gas canisters to make student protesters disperse, May 4, 1970. When the tear gas failed to break up the demonstration, some National Guardsmen fired their rifles at the students.

War Protest Turns Deadly

TERROR IN THE SKIES

Terrorists are individuals who try to spread fear, so that governments and societies will give in to their demands. Through shocking acts of violence (or the threat of violence), terrorists hope to achieve their political goals.

In the late 1960s, terrorists began hijacking airplanes. Using weapons they had smuggled aboard, a small group of hijackers could take control of a plane. They would order the pilot to land, often in a place other than the plane's intended destination. Then, holding the passengers hostage, the hijackers would state their demands. Sometimes they wanted money. Other times, they demanded the release of members of their terrorist group who were being held prisoner. But always, the hijackers got publicity for their cause.

Many hijackings were carried out by members of Palestinian terrorist groups. The Palestinians are Arab people who lived in Palestine. Palestine is the area in which the Jewish state of Israel was established. Hundreds of thousands of Palestinians fled from their homes during the war that took place after Israel's founding in 1948. Many of these Palestinians ended up in poor, crowded refugee camps in neighboring Arab countries. The Six-Day War in June 1967 created more Palestinian refugees. Also, because Israel occupied the West Bank and Gaza Strip, more than a million Palestinians living in these areas came under Israeli rule in 1967.

Passengers who had been held hostage by Palestinian terrorists are released in Frankfurt, West Germany, after German commandos regained control of the airplane, October 1977. During the 1970s, many different terrorist groups hijacked airplanes. This was often done to draw attention to the group's cause. In addition to Palestinians, groups from Germany, the Philippines, South Asia, the Balkans, and Japan hijacked airplanes during the decade.

Palestinian terrorist groups wanted to destroy Israel. The most famous of these groups was the Palestine Liberation Organization (PLO), headed by Yasir Arafat. But not all Palestinians shared the goal of destroying Israel. Many simply wanted to be able to return to their land, or to see the creation of a Palestinian state.

By the early 1970s, airline hijackings were a major problem around the world. Government officials had few choices once a plane had been hijacked. They could order soldiers or special police units to storm the aircraft. But many hostages might die before the hijackers were killed or captured. Government officials could also choose to meet some of the terrorists' demands in exchange for the release of the hostages. Unfortunately, this might encourage future hijackings.

Palestinian leader Yasir Arafat (1929–2004) makes a speech, 1972. Arafat's Palestine Liberation Organization (PLO) secretly supported airplane hijackings and terror attacks throughout the 1970s.

An Israeli woman who was among the Entebbe hostages is greeted by her family after her rescue.

By the mid-1970s, governments had increased airport security to try to prevent hijackings. They installed X-ray machines in airports. These machines could reveal weapons hidden inside luggage.

Unlike some other countries, Israel always refused to meet hijackers' demands. On June 27, 1976, Palestinian terrorists hijacked a French airliner that had many Israelis aboard. They took the plane to Entebbe, in the African country of Uganda. Uganda's dictator, Idi Amin, supported the terrorists. The terrorists threatened to kill the passengers if more than fifty Palestinian terrorists being held prisoner in five countries were not released. On July 3, 1976, a special unit of Israeli soldiers took off from Israel and flew more than two thousand miles to Entebbe. They fought off Ugandan soldiers, killed all the hijackers, and rescued more than one hundred passengers. Three hostages and the leader of the Israeli soldiers also died in the daring raid.

ANTIWAR SENTIMENT PEAKS

Many Americans opposed the Vietnam War. As the war dragged on into the early 1970s, the number of people who thought U.S. troops should leave Vietnam grew. Two news stories in the early 1970s fanned public outrage over the war.

First, Americans learned of an incident that had occurred earlier in Vietnam. In March 1968, U.S. soldiers had attacked the village of My Lai. They killed up to five hundred unarmed civilians there. An army officer named William Calley led the soldiers. In 1971, he went on trial for the killings at My Lai. He was found guilty. People were shocked by the grisly details of the My Lai massacre. They were also angry that army officers had tried to keep the massacre a secret.

Another secret about the war was revealed in 1971. Newspaper reporters learned of the Pentagon Papers. The Pentagon Papers were top-secret government files. They showed that the U.S. government had sometimes lied

American soldiers defend a fire base—a camp that provided artillery support for the infantry—in Vietnam, 1972. As the number of American casualties grew, people began to turn against the Vietnam War.

The *New York Times* continued publishing articles based on the secret Pentagon papers after it was given the green light by the U.S. Supreme Court in July 1971.

about the Vietnam War. For example, top government officials had insisted for years that America was winning the war. But, as the Pentagon Papers revealed, many officials did not believe the war could be won.

President Nixon tried to keep newspapers from printing the Pentagon Papers. However, the U.S. Supreme Court ruled that they could. The release of the Pentagon Papers fueled further antiwar sentiment. By 1973, seven out of ten Americans opposed the war.

LOWERING THE VOTING AGE

The Vietnam War played a part in the lowering of America's voting age. Men as young as eighteen were being drafted into the army. Yet Americans had to be at least twenty-one to vote. Many people said it was unfair to expect someone to fight in a war if that person did not have the right to help choose the country's leaders. In 1971, the Twenty-sixth Amendment to the Constitution set the voting age throughout America at eighteen. Two years later, in 1973, the military draft was ended.

Antiwar Sentiment Peaks

U.S. President Richard Nixon (left) and Soviet leader Leonid Brezhnev sign a treaty that limited the number of nuclear weapons each country could possess. The Strategic Arms Limitation Talks (SALT) treaty, signed in Moscow in 1972, was one of the benefits of *détente*. A second SALT treaty between the two countries was signed in 1979.

THE COLD WAR THAWS

The Cold War was a fierce rivalry between the United States and the Soviet Union. It started after World War II and lasted for decades. Neither side trusted the other. Both nations feared a sneak attack. In 1962, the United States and the Soviet Union had come dangerously close to a nuclear war after the Soviets placed missiles in Cuba. By the 1970s, both sides were eager to reduce the tension.

Despite *détente*, the Cold War continued during the 1970s. The United States and Soviet Union each took sides in conflicts in Africa, the Middle East, and Asia. When a civil war broke out in Angola during 1975, the U.S. provided money and weapons to the UNITA party led by Jonas Savimbi (pictured). The Soviet Union and its allies supported MPLA, a communist party in Angola.

The Apollo-Soyuz crew included (from left) American astronauts Donald "Deke" Slayton, Tom Stafford, and Vance Brand, and Russian cosmonauts Aleksey Leonov and Valeriy Kubasov.

U.S. and Soviet leaders began holding talks. They discussed key issues such as nuclear weapons and human rights. Both nations agreed to limit the number of nuclear missiles they kept. They also agreed to trade more goods with one another. The Soviet Union bought large amounts of U.S. wheat. This new spirit of cooperation was called *détente*. It is a French word meaning to relax or to ease.

The U.S. and Soviet space programs also joined forces. They launched a joint mission in space. In 1975, orbiting U.S. and Soviet spacecraft docked together. Astronauts from both countries shook hands while floating high above Earth. The Apollo-Soyuz mission offered hope for better relations between the two superpowers.

But the era of détente did not last long. By the end of the 1970s, America and the Soviet Union were once again enemies. In 1979, Soviet troops invaded the neighboring country of Afghanistan. America aided Afghan rebels who were fighting the Soviets. Both superpowers began building up their military forces. The fear and hatred of the Cold War returned.

NIXON GOES TO CHINA

In 1949, China became a communist country. It was called the People's Republic of China. Shortly after, U.S. and Chinese soldiers clashed in the Korean War. In the two decades that followed, America and China remained wary of each other. The United States did not even recognize the People's Republic as the legitimate government of China. Then, in 1972, the two countries took steps toward friendship. President Nixon made a historic trip to China. He met with Chinese leader Mao Zedong. They agreed to peaceful relations between their nations.

President Nixon's trip made world headlines. No U.S. president had ever before gone to the People's Republic of China. Although not a superpower, China was the most populous nation in the world. Nixon's visit worried the Soviet Union. A friendship with China, which borders the Soviet Union, would give America an advantage in the Cold War. This concern spurred Soviet interest in détente with the United States.

Chinese leader Mao Zedong (1893–1976) shakes hands with President Nixon, February 1972. Nixon's success at improving American relations with its two greatest enemies, China and the Soviet Union, is considered one of his most important accomplishments.

The Cold War Thaws

TRAGEDY IN THE MUSIC WORLD

Rock music of the early 1970s had a raw and heavy sound. Musicians thrilled crowds with frantic, intense performances.

Some musicians lived wild lifestyles offstage as well. In 1970 and 1971, three of rock's top performers died from drug abuse. They were Jimi Hendrix, Janis Joplin, and Jim Morrison.

Jimi Hendrix grew up in Seattle, Washington. From an early age, he showed amazing skills with the guitar. His music was fiery and dramatic. Hendrix is best remembered for his hit song "Purple Haze." At Woodstock in 1969, he performed the national anthem with his guitar.

During the early 1970s, three of the most popular rock musicians died because of drug and alcohol abuse. The unique guitar style of Jimi Hendrix (1942–1970) continues to influence popular music today.

A year later, Jimi Hendrix died of drug-related causes. He was only twenty-seven years old.

Janis Joplin was born in Texas in 1943. She ran away from home at age seventeen to become a singer. She had a powerful voice. Joplin became a star after performing in the Monterey Pop Festival in 1967. She died three years later from a heroin overdose.

Jim Morrison was the lead singer for a band called the Doors. The Florida native also wrote poetry. The Doors had an explosive sound. Their first album contained the number-one hit "Light My Fire." In 1971, Jim Morrison was in France when he died, probably from an overdose of heroin. Like Joplin and Hendrix, he was just twenty-seven years old.

Tragedy in the Music World

TERRORISTS STRIKE THE OLYMPICS

The Olympic flag and national flags fly at half-mast during a memorial service for eleven Israeli athletes murdered at the 1972 Munich Olympics.

*T*he Olympic Games have long been a celebration of sports and friendship. Athletes from across the globe gather at one place. They compete and represent their nations. In 1972, the Summer Olympics were held in Munich, West Germany. The event began with much fanfare. Before it ended, there would be great sadness. A terrorist attack killed eleven athletes.

A Palestinian terrorist group known as Black September carried out the attack. On the morning of September 5, 1972, eight men from Black September slipped into the Olympic Village in Munich. They broke into apartments occupied by members of the Israeli wrestling and weight-lifting teams. Two of the Israelis tried to bar a door. They were shot and killed. Nine others were taken hostage.

A masked member of the Palestinian group Black September appears on a balcony of the building where the terrorists held members of the Israeli Olympic team hostage, September 5, 1972.

Around the world, television viewers watched in horror. Overnight, the joy of the Olympics gave way to a deadly crisis. The terrorists made their demands. They wanted hundreds of their comrades released from Israeli prisons. Israel refused. As the day wore on, German police officers planned a rescue attempt. Their plan was ruined when TV news cameras showed them sneaking into position. The terrorists saw the police on live television and warned them away.

The terrorists demanded to be flown out of Germany. Two helicopters carried them and their hostages to a nearby airport to board a jet. At the airport, German police made another rescue attempt. Snipers tried to shoot the terrorists as they crossed the runway. The terrorists shot back. They also killed the nine remaining hostages. The fighting at the airport raged. A German police officer was killed. So were five of the terrorists. The other three were captured.

In the wake of the bloodshed, Olympic officials debated canceling the rest of the Munich Games. They decided against it. Most people felt that quitting would be a victory for terrorism. Instead, a memorial service was held to honor the eleven Israeli victims. The Olympics then somberly continued.

Most nations condemned Black September's attack on the Olympics. Even some other radical groups decried it. In the months that followed the Munich attack, Israeli agents hunted down and killed members of Black September. By 1974, the terrorist organization was no longer operating.

A ceremony for the eleven slain Israeli athletes in Tel Aviv, Israel. Each athlete's name is written in Hebrew on the memorial.

RECORD-SETTING ATHLETES

Terrorism spoiled the festive mood of the 1972 Olympics. Yet there were still some amazing athletic feats. An American swimmer named Mark Spitz set four world records. He also earned seven gold medals. No Olympic athlete had ever won so many gold medals at once.

The twenty-two-year-old Spitz came from California. He had been competing as a swimmer since the age of eight. As a teen, Spitz set several world records. He specialized in the freestyle and butterfly events. At the Munich Olympics, Spitz was in peak form. He won four solo events. He also led the U.S. swim team to victory in three relay events.

Mark Spitz was not the only record-setter of the 1970s. As Spitz swam, a baseball player named Hank Aaron chased the all-time

American swimmer Mark Spitz holds several of the gold medals he won at the 1972 Olympic Games. His record of seven gold medals in a single Games lasted until 2008. It was broken by another American swimmer, Michael Phelps, who won eight medals at the Beijing Olympics.

Hank Aaron blasts the 714th home run of his career, April 4, 1974. Aaron was one of the greatest baseball players of all time. In addition to setting a new record for career home runs, he drove in more runs (2,297) than any other player. His 3,771 hits were the second-highest total in baseball history at the time he retired.

home run record. Aaron was born in Alabama in 1934. He broke into the major leagues in 1954. The outfielder quickly established himself as a consistent .300 hitter.

On baseball's opening day in 1974, Aaron tied Babe Ruth's career record of 714 home runs. Two games after that, on April 8, 1974, Hank Aaron blasted his 715th homer to become baseball's all-time home run king. He finished his career in 1976 with 755 homers.

Tennis star Billie Jean King returns a shot during an exhibition match against a male player named Bobby Riggs. King won the 1973 match, which was called "The Battle of the Sexes." At the time, many women considered King's victory a significant moment in the women's rights movement. They believed it proved that women could compete with men in many fields.

U.S. Troops Leave Vietnam

Since 1965, U.S. combat troops had been fighting bloody battles in Vietnam. Many Americans despised the Vietnam War. For years, they had been demanding an end to U.S. involvement. Finally, in 1973, the last American combat soldiers came home.

President Nixon oversaw America's withdrawal from Vietnam. He knew that North Vietnam would not give up its bid to take over South Vietnam. American troops held the North Vietnamese army at bay. However, the

Young men from South Vietnam march from an American-run training camp in the early 1970s. The Nixon administration developed a plan to increase the strength of the Army of South Vietnam. This would allow the United States to withdraw its combat troops from the Vietnam War.

American soldiers could not stay and defend South Vietnam forever. Nixon decided to focus on helping South Vietnam build up its own army. That would enable U.S. forces to leave.

America withdrew from the war slowly. The number of U.S. troops in Vietnam reached its peak in 1968. The troop level was reduced in 1969, and it declined steadily over the next four years. Meanwhile, South Vietnam's army received weapons and training. It was not enough, however. In 1975, North Vietnam conquered South Vietnam. The two became a single, communist nation. More than 58,000 Americans had died in the Vietnam War. Millions of Vietnamese were killed.

A North Vietnamese Army tank breaks through an iron gate around the presidential palace in Saigon, the capital of South Vietnam, April 1975. In early 1973, the United States had signed a peace agreement with North Vietnam and brought American troops home. However, the treaty did not end the fighting. In 1975 troops from North Vietnam conquered South Vietnam and reunited the country under communist rule.

A section of the Vietnam Veterans Memorial in Washington, D.C. The black granite memorial, sometimes known as "the Wall," lists the names of 58,256 Americans who were killed during the Vietnam War.

NATION ENDURES OIL CRISIS

Oil is essential to a modern society. Oil heats people's homes. It powers factories. Cars run on gas made from oil. In the early 1970s, Americans faced a sudden oil shortage. It created a major energy crisis.

Much of the world's oil comes from the Middle East. Oil drilled in Arab countries is shipped around the globe. In 1973, the Arab nations stopped shipping oil to the United States. They wished to punish America for its

An oil refinery in Saudi Arabia, circa 1974. Arab countries like Saudi Arabia, Iraq, and Kuwait possess a large share of the world's petroleum. In the 1970s, the Arab states tried to use their control of this important resource to influence American policy in the Middle East.

Israeli tanks cross the Sinai Desert during the Yom Kippur War, October 1973. Israel was able to outfight two larger Arab countries, Syria and Egypt, during the conflict. Israel's success was due in part to weapons and technology that the United States had provided. American support of Israel angered many Arabs, leading to the oil embargo.

support of Israel during the Yom Kippur War. That three-week conflict was fought in October 1973, after Egypt and Syria attacked Israel. The Arab countries also stopped shipping oil to other countries that supported Israel.

The lack of oil caused many problems in the United States. It became very costly to heat a home or run a business. Some factories laid off workers. There was also a shortage of gas. Drivers were allowed to fill up their cars only on certain days. Lines at gas stations were sometimes blocks long. In March 1974, the Arab nations started shipping oil again. The crisis passed. However, America's need for foreign oil would cause many more problems in the future.

Signs like this were common during the 1973–1974 oil crisis in the United States. The price of gasoline rose sharply, and shortages were common.

President Nixon waves as he departs from the White House in disgrace, August 9, 1974.

PRESIDENT NIXON RESIGNS

In 1974, President Richard Nixon resigned from office. Never before had a U.S. president quit without finishing his term. Nixon quit because of a scandal. It was known as Watergate. The scandal shook the public's faith in its government.

Watergate began with a break-in on June 17, 1972. Five men broke into the Watergate building in Washington, D.C. They raided the offices of the

The *Washington Post* won a Pulitzer Prize in 1973 for its investigative reporting on the Watergate burglary. A series of stories by *Post* reporters Bob Woodward (right) and Carl Bernstein led Congress to investigate the president's involvement in Watergate.

A political cartoon from 1974 shows Nixon tangled in a spider's web as recording tapes dangle next to him. Tapes of conversations in the White House showed that Nixon had ordered members of his staff to block an investigation into the 1972 Watergate Hotel break-in.

Democratic Party. They wanted to find information that would discredit the Democrats. The burglars were caught. Investigators later learned that the men were working for advisers of President Nixon. Nixon and his advisers were members of the Republican Party.

As news reporters and the U.S. Congress dug further into the Watergate break-in, they uncovered more illegal acts. The president himself was involved. Although he did not order the Watergate break-in, Nixon tried to cover up the fact that his aides had hired the burglars. Secret tape recordings from the president's office proved his guilt. Congress moved to impeach the president. If an impeachment vote passed the U.S. House of Representatives, Nixon would face a trial in the U.S. Senate. If convicted there, he would be removed from office. To avoid that, the president resigned. He left the White House on August 9, 1974.

The Watergate scandal was a disgraceful chapter in U.S. history. It made many Americans distrustful of their leaders. Yet it also showed that in the United States, no one—not even the president—is above the law.

When Richard Nixon resigned in August 1974, Gerald R. Ford became the thirty-eighth president of the United States. It was the first time in U.S. history that a person became the nation's chief executive without being elected president or vice president.

Nixon's first vice president had been Spiro T. Agnew. In October 1973, however, Agnew resigned from office. He was facing criminal charges of bribery and tax fraud. To fill the office of vice president, Nixon nominated Ford, a longtime congressman from Michigan. The U.S. Senate and House of Representatives voted to confirm Ford, as required by the Twenty-fifth Amendment to the Constitution.

In 1976, Ford ran for president against the Democratic nominee, Jimmy Carter. Carter was a former governor of Georgia. He was an outsider to Washington politics. In the aftermath of the Watergate scandal, this was an advantage. In November, Carter defeated Gerald Ford to win the presidency.

Gerald Ford (1913–2006) is sworn in as president by Supreme Court Chief Justice Warren Burger, August 9, 1974. In September 1974, Ford pardoned Richard Nixon for any crimes the former president might have committed while in office. Many Americans were outraged by the pardon. It probably contributed to Ford's defeat in the 1976 presidential election.

AN UNELECTED PRESIDENT

HOLLYWOOD'S BIGGEST HITS

DVDs did not yet exist in the 1970s. Video players, known as VCRs, were new, and few families owned one. People flocked to theaters to see movies. Hollywood scored some of its biggest hits during this decade.

The Godfather debuted in 1972. It was based on the novel by Mario Puzo. The Godfather told the story of an Italian-American crime family, the Corleones. It was a violent but intriguing movie. It received many awards. These included the Academy Award for Best Picture. Today, some people still consider it one of the best films ever made. Two successful sequels would follow, in 1974 and 1990.

Jaws was also based on a novel. Peter Benchley's book was about a giant killer shark. Hollywood released Jaws in 1975. Its eerie music and gripping images thrilled moviegoers. Some viewers found Jaws so scary that they avoided the beach that summer.

This scene from The Godfather features Marlon Brando (right) as Vito Corleone and Al Pacino (seated) as his son, Michael. The violent movie won three Academy Awards. It is considered one of the greatest films of all time.

The success of *Jaws* changed the way movie studios released their big-budget films. Universal Pictures allowed hundreds of theaters across the country to begin showing *Jaws* on the same day. This strategy, known as "wide release," enabled *Jaws* to become the first movie to earn more than $100 million at the box office.

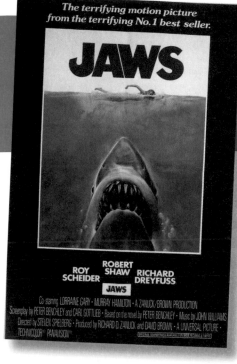

The original *Star Wars* movie came out in 1977. It was a science fiction film by George Lucas. *Star Wars* featured hero Luke Skywalker and villain Darth Vader. There were also aliens, lovable robots, and dazzling space battles. *Star Wars* earned more money than any previous film in Hollywood history. The movie also created a marketing frenzy. People snapped up Star Wars books, action figures, costumes, and other merchandise. Eventually, six more movies in the series would be released.

Amazing special effects made the original *Star Wars* film (later subtitled *A New Hope*) incredibly popular after it was released in May 1977. Other films that continued and expanded on the original story include *The Empire Strikes Back* (1980), *Return of the Jedi* (1983), *The Phantom Menace* (1999), *Attack of the Clones* (2002), *Revenge of the Sith* (2005), and an animated film, *The Clone Wars* (2008).

AMERICA CELEBRATES ITS BICENTENNIAL

A two-hundred-year anniversary is called a bicentennial. In 1976, the United States celebrated its bicentennial. Two hundred years earlier, America had declared its independence from Britain.

During the American Revolution, colonial leaders adopted the Declaration of Independence in this building in Philadelphia on July 4, 1776. Independence Hall, as the structure became known, was the site of many events during the nation's bicentennial year, 1976.

President Ford initiates the ringing of bicentennial bells across the nation while on the flight deck of the aircraft carrier USS *Forrestal* in New York harbor. With him is Bicentennial Administration director John Warner. The Bicentennial Administration was a government agency created to coordinate bicentennial events throughout the country during 1976.

The bicentennial celebration lasted for months. People wore red, white, and blue clothing. They flew the American flag. The U.S. Mint issued special coins. The U.S. Postal Service issued special stamps. A surge of patriotism swept across the country. People once again felt proud of their nation.

The revelry peaked on July 4, 1976. In Washington, D.C., President Gerald Ford led a huge celebration. It featured fireworks and music. In New York harbor, a fleet of old-fashioned sailing ships gathered. People in Boston reenacted the Boston Tea Party.

Nearly every town and city in America held its own special celebration. There were picnics, fireworks, and parades. The bicentennial was an important cultural event. It brought the nation together during a difficult time.

Special quarters were minted for the bicentennial observation. They bore the dates "1776–1976" on one side. On the other side, the quarters featured a special design showing a drummer in the Continental Army. A torch circled by thirteen stars represented the original American colonies that had declared their independence from Great Britain.

Disco Dancing and Funky Fashion

A new type of music emerged in the 1970s. It was called disco. Its fast beat made disco music ideal for dancing. Nightclubs filled with patrons eager to try the latest disco steps. A mirrored ball usually hung overhead. It splashed patterns of light across a colorful dance floor.

The film *Saturday Night Fever*, released in 1977, came to symbolize the disco era. It starred John Travolta as a poor but talented dancer. Many scenes showed people doing disco dances like the Hustle. *Saturday Night Fever* featured songs by popular disco artists. These included the Bee Gees as well as KC and the Sunshine Band. The film's soundtrack quickly became a top-selling album.

Fashion of the 1970s was unusual. When going out to dance, men often wore a two- or three-piece outfit called a leisure suit.

The 1977 motion picture *Saturday Night Fever* illustrated the power of the disco craze.

It consisted of a jacket, dress pants, and sometimes a vest. White was a favorite color. Plaid was also considered stylish. Women typically wore blouses with skirts or slacks. Most dress shirts had wide collars.

Clothing was often made from an artificial fiber called polyester. Men as well as women wore platform shoes to make them look taller. The disco era did not last long. It drew to a close as the decade ended.

Patrons dance at a disco in Washington, D.C., during the mid-1970s.

U.S. president Jimmy Carter stands between Egypt's president, Anwar Sadat (1918–1981) and Israel's prime minister, Menachem Begin (1913–1992), on the White House lawn, March 26, 1979. Their handshake marked a historic moment in the history of the Middle East. For the first time, an Arab country had agreed to peace with Israel.

PROGRESS IN THE MIDDLE EAST

For decades, Egypt and Israel were fierce enemies. Their hatred added to the tension of the Middle East. Then, in 1978, leaders from Egypt and Israel came together. They traveled to the United States. With help from President Jimmy Carter, they created a peace treaty. It was a rare moment of progress in the Arab-Israeli conflict.

In November 1977, Sadat spoke to Israel's legislature, the Knesset, about Egypt's willingness for peace. Sadat's visit to Israel was a dramatic gesture that surprised many people and made the peace process possible.

Anwar Sadat was Egypt's president. As a young man, he had been a soldier. Later, he joined the Egyptian government. In the 1960s, he twice served as vice president. In 1967, Israeli troops soundly beat his nation's army in the Six-Day War. Sadat was shocked. He vowed to regain the land Egypt lost during that war. As president in 1973, Sadat launched a new war against Israel. He tried to capture the lost territory, but failed. In the years that followed, Sadat changed his views. He grew to believe that peace with Israel was the only answer.

Menachem Begin was active in Israeli politics from his country's founding. He served in parliament for many years. In 1977, Begin became Israel's prime minister. Like Sadat of Egypt, Begin desired peace. However, the two men did not get along well with each other. They needed someone to help them

In September 1978, President Carter secretly brought Sadat and Begin together at Camp David, a presidential retreat in Maryland. The leaders met for twelve days at Camp David. There, they worked out the framework for a peace treaty between Egypt and Israel.

Sadat, Carter, and Begin sign the Camp David Accords at a White House ceremony, September 17, 1978. The Accords formed the basis of the 1979 peace treaty between Israel and Egypt. The peace has lasted to the present day.

overcome their differences. U.S. president Jimmy Carter offered to help. He invited them to Camp David, the presidential retreat in Maryland.

At Camp David, President Carter worked tirelessly. For twelve days, he talked with Sadat and Begin. He persuaded them to reach an agreement. The Camp David Accords proved that peace was possible in the Middle East. It ended the ongoing state of war between Egypt and Israel. The two countries began normal diplomatic relations. For their efforts, Sadat and Begin received the 1978 Nobel Peace Prize.

Some Arab nations were angry at Egypt for making peace with Israel. They broke off relations with Egypt. They also kicked Egypt out of the Arab League, an organization of Arab states. In 1981, Egyptian terrorists shot and killed Anwar Sadat.

MASS SUICIDE IN JONESTOWN

A group of people with unusual religious beliefs is sometimes called a cult. Typically, cult members are strongly devoted to their leader and will do almost anything the leader asks of them. Jim Jones was the leader of a cult called the Peoples Temple. In 1978, Jones convinced his followers to kill themselves.

Jim Jones was born in Indiana in 1931. As a young man, Jones created his own religion based on communist ideas such as the equal sharing of property. He attracted many followers. Eventually, Jones moved his cult from California to South America. He built a camp in the nation of Guyana. The camp was named Jonestown after its founder.

Jim Jones (1931–1978) created the Peoples Temple in the mid-1950s. By 1978, the cult had thousands of members, most of whom lived in California.

Congressman Leo Ryan (1925–1978) of California attempted to raise awareness about the dangers of religious cults. In addition to the Peoples Temple, Ryan criticized organizations like the Unification Church and the Church of Scientology.

U.S. officials began hearing stories of abuse and suffering at Jonestown. Congressman Leo Ryan flew to Jonestown to investigate. Jim Jones's armed guards shot and killed Ryan and several other visitors. After the murders, Jones told his followers that soldiers would come to attack them. He said that suicide was their only way of escape. More than nine hundred people followed his instructions. They drank poison. Their dead bodies littered the ground. Jim Jones shot himself in the head or was shot by an aide. The mass suicide at Jonestown startled the world.

This aerial shot of the Peoples Temple compound in Guyana shows the bodies of cult members who participated in the mass suicide at Jonestown.

TRAGEDY AVOIDED AT THREE MILE ISLAND

Power plants make electricity. Some power plants make electricity by burning coal or oil. Nuclear power plants are different. They use an element called uranium to generate power. Nuclear power is very efficient and, unlike power from oil and coal, does not create greenhouse gases. But there is a danger. Uranium emits harmful radiation. It must be carefully contained at the plant. In 1979, a large amount of radiation nearly escaped from a nuclear power plant.

On March 28, 1979, the nuclear power plant at Three Mile Island in central Pennsylvania became dangerously overheated. Some radiation escaped from the plant before it could be shut down.

Inspectors from the Nuclear Regulatory Commission prepare to check the plant at Three Mile Island for high levels of radiation, April 1979. It took years and cost nearly $1 billion to make the contaminated plant safe.

The crisis happened in Pennsylvania. The nuclear power plant at Three Mile Island had an accident. A valve on a pipe got stuck open. Water that was supposed to cool the nuclear reactor escaped. As a result, the plant's uranium got very hot and began to melt. There was a chance that the plant could start leaking radiation. People in nearby towns feared for their safety. They began to leave.

After five tense days, plant workers managed to halt the damage. President Jimmy Carter tried to calm people down. He personally went to the accident site to show that there was no longer any danger. Investigators found that a small amount of radiation did escape during the crisis. However, it was not enough to cause harm. Part of the plant was destroyed by the accident. The rest of it reopened after repairs. The Three Mile Island nuclear power plant is still operating today.

The crowd at an anti-nuclear power rally in Harrisburg. The near-disaster at Three Mile Island raised fears about the safety of nuclear power. As a result, construction of new nuclear plants dropped sharply during the 1980s and 1990s.

Tragedy Avoided at Three Mile Island

TECH FIRSTS

*T*he 1970s saw early versions of some electronic items that are well known today. The multibillion-dollar video game industry began humbly in 1972. That year, a company named Atari released the first commercially successful video game. Called Pong, it bore a vague resemblance to tennis. By today's standards, Pong's graphics would be laughable. Players hit a square "ball" with rectangular "rackets" that could move only up and down on the two-dimensional screen.

People play Space Invaders on an Atari home video game system. Space Invaders was released in 1978 as one of the first arcade video games. The Atari 2600 system pictured on top of the television first appeared on the market in 1977.

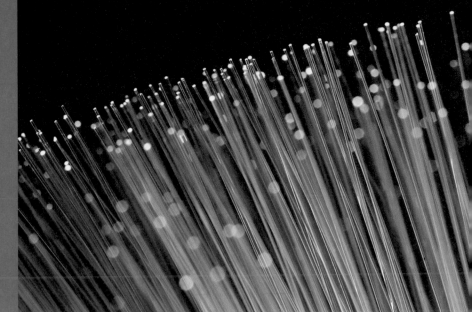

In 1970, the Corning Glass Works created the first optical fibers capable of carrying a light signal over a long distance. By the end of the decade, optical fiber cables were replacing copper wires in telephone systems. Today, optical fibers have many other uses, from computer networks to medical procedures.

The first computers designed for use by individuals made their appearance in the mid-1970s. In 1975, a company called MITS created the Altair 8800. It cost only about four hundred dollars. But it came as a kit—the buyer had to assemble the machine. Soon, other companies began selling fully assembled personal computers. In 1976, the first Apple computer went on sale. The next year, the company released a new model, the Apple II. It quickly became the most popular personal computer. By the end of the decade, Apple II computers could be found in millions of homes, offices, and schools.

Today, many people like to listen to music on their MP3 players as they work out, walk, or ride buses and trains. The first personal stereo system a person could carry around came out in 1979. Made by Sony, it was called the Walkman. It played cassette tapes.

Apple Computer co-founder Steve Jobs poses with an Apple II computer, late 1970s.

AMERICANS HELD HOSTAGE IN IRAN

Iran is a country in the Middle East. It is one of the world's top oil producers. For decades, the United States and Iran were allies. That changed in 1979. Iran underwent a revolution. Its new leaders despised the United States, which had supported Iran's hated shah, or king. In November 1979, American citizens working at the U.S. embassy in Iran's capital were taken hostage. A fourteen-month crisis ensued.

Islamic religious leader Ayatollah Ruhollah Khomeini (1900–1989) led a revolution in Iran during the late 1970s. In early 1979, Iranians overthrew the country's government. By the end of that year, Khomeini was the country's new ruler.

Before the Iranian revolution, Shah Mohammad Reza Pahlavi ruled the country. The shah was very unpopular with his people. He relied on threats and torture

Mohammad Reza Pahlavi (1919–1980), shah of Iran, and his daughter Princess Farah, are pictured during a visit to the United States. The shah was forced to flee from Iran in January 1979 and died in exile the next year.

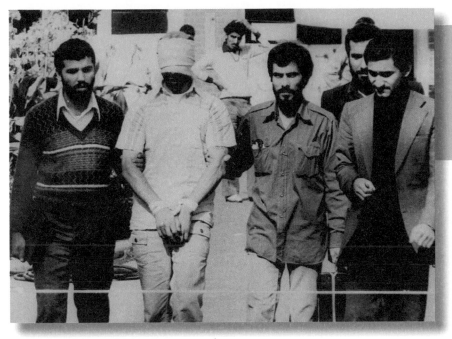

to stay in power. Iranians also disliked his close ties with America. Over time, many Iranians came to believe that Iran's religious leaders should be in charge of the country. (Most Iranians follow the religion of Islam.) An Islamic scholar named Ruhollah Khomeini led the move toward revolution. As protesters filled the streets, the shah fled. Khomeini took control of Iran.

Although the shah no longer held power, Iranians still hated him. They became outraged when the ex-leader was allowed to enter the United States. Protesters stormed the U.S. embassy in Iran. They took fifty-three Americans hostage. The U.S. government demanded the release of its citizens. Iran stubbornly refused. The embassy workers would be held prisoner for more than a year.

Freed American hostages wave to a crowd in Germany before boarding an airplane for the United States. Iran released the hostages on January 20, 1981, after holding them for 444 days.

Americans Held Hostage in Iran

The flag of the communist Khalq Party flies over the presidential palace in Kabul, Afghanistan, April 1979. After the Afghan communists seized power, they asked the Soviet Union to help them control the country. In August, the Soviet Red Army invaded Afghanistan to support the communist government.

SOVIET TROOPS INVADE AFGHANISTAN

Afghanistan is a rugged land in southwest Asia. It has many mountains and deserts. In 1979, a much larger neighbor invaded Afghanistan. The Soviet Union sent in tanks and troops. A nine-year war followed. The Soviet invasion of Afghanistan had a major impact on world events.

Soviet infantry vehicles move through Afghanistan on patrol. During the late 1970s, the U.S.S.R.'s Red Army was one of the world's most powerful fighting forces. However, the Soviet troops were unable to maintain peace in Afghanistan. Fighting continued there for a decade.

A crowd watches the opening ceremony of the twenty-second Olympic Games, July 1980. Because of the Soviet invasion of Afghanistan, the United States and sixty other countries refused to participate in the Moscow Games.

For decades, the Soviet Union had meddled in Afghan affairs. In 1978, a pro-Soviet communist party seized power in Afghanistan. Soon, however, Afghans rose up to get rid of the new government. By 1979, Afghanistan's communist government was in trouble. It called for help from the Soviet Union. Soviet leaders responded by ordering a large invasion. Soviet soldiers, tanks, and helicopters rushed across the Afghan border. They quickly seized the capital of Kabul and other cities. Afghan fighters were unable to stop the Soviets. The poorly armed fighters fled to the mountains.

The United States protested the Soviet invasion of Afghanistan. America and the Soviet Union were still Cold War rivals. U.S. officials feared that the Soviets might be planning more invasions in Asia. President Carter took steps to show his ire. He canceled all sales of U.S. wheat to the Soviet Union.

The 1980 Summer Olympics were scheduled to take place in Moscow, the Soviet capital. Carter declared that American athletes would not take part in those Olympics.

The U.S. government took another step. It secretly began helping the Afghan rebels hiding in the mountains. The rebels started receiving shipments of weapons and supplies. Before long, they were able to fight back against the Soviets. The rebels were devoted believers in Islam. They viewed their struggle against the Soviets as a holy war. The rebels called themselves *mujahideen*, or holy warriors. After years of bitter fighting, they would defeat the Soviet army—with consequences that are still felt today.

Members of a *mujahideen* group pose in the mountains of eastern Afghanistan. They are holding weapons that were secretly provided by the United States. The *mujahideen* resistance drove the Red Army out of Afghanistan in 1989.

LOOKING AHEAD

The decade 1970–1979 was a tough time for the United States. The nation endured defeat in Vietnam. Watergate caused many people to doubt their government. From Three Mile Island to Jonestown, there seemed to be nothing but bad news. At the end of the decade, the American economy was struggling. Companies were closing and people were losing their jobs. The many problems created an uneasy sense of doubt. Some people wondered whether America's power was waning.

In November 1980, Ronald Reagan was elected president of the United States. His administration put bold new political and economic policies into place. These helped America to bounce back from its troubles of the 1970s. The economy improved, creating new jobs. The space shuttle made its first flight. Personal computers became available. America proved it was still a world leader in technology.

Yet the United States also experienced troubles during the 1980s. A deadly disease called AIDS killed millions of people. A new drug known as "crack" became the source of much suffering and violence in American cities. The gap between wealthy and poor Americans grew wider during the 1980s. In 1987, the U.S. stock market crashed. Meanwhile, wars raged around the globe.

As the decade ended, the Cold War began to thaw. Soviet leader Mikhail Gorbachev tried to overhaul the Soviet government and economy. He also wanted to improve relations with the United States. But Gorbachev's reforms led to many changes. Soon, the Soviet Union would break apart, and the United States would be the world's only superpower.

Ronald and Nancy Reagan dance during an inaugural ball, January 1981. As president of the United States from 1981 to 1989, Reagan implemented policies that reshaped the nation and the world.

CHRONOLOGY

1970—The Kent State shootings take place in May. Musicians Jimi Hendrix and Janis Joplin die from drug abuse. The U.S. Army charges fourteen officers with trying to cover up the My Lai massacre.

1971—Newspapers publish the top-secret Pentagon Papers about the Vietnam War. Rock singer Jim Morrison dies in July, probably from a heroin overdose.

1972—In February, Richard Nixon becomes the first U.S. president to visit the People's Republic of China. In September, terrorists kill eleven Israeli athletes at the Munich Olympics.

1973—The last U.S. combat troops leave Vietnam. In October, the Yom Kippur War is fought in the Middle East. Arab nations temporarily stop selling oil to America, creating an energy crisis.

1974—Hank Aaron breaks Babe Ruth's career home-run record. President Nixon resigns in August because of the Watergate scandal. Gerald Ford becomes president.

1975—North Vietnam conquers South Vietnam. In July, U.S. and Soviet spacecraft conduct a joint mission. The hit film *Jaws* is released.

1976—America celebrates its bicentennial anniversary. In July, Israeli soldiers rescue the passengers of a hijacked jetliner in Entebbe, Uganda. Jimmy Carter is elected president in November.

1977—Egypt's Anwar Sadat and Israel's Menachem Begin meet for the first time to discuss peace. The films *Saturday Night Fever* and *Star Wars* debut.

1978—President Carter helps negotiate the Camp David Accords between Israel and Egypt. In November, more than nine hundred followers of Jim Jones commit suicide in Jonestown, Guyana.

1979—The Three Mile Island nuclear accident occurs in March. In November, fifty-three American embassy workers are taken hostage in Iran. The Soviet Union invades Afghanistan in December.

GLOSSARY

bicentennial—Relating to a two-hundredth anniversary.

communist—A follower of a type of political and economic system in which all citizens are supposed to share work and property equally.

crisis—A situation that has reached a critical and often dangerous stage.

cult—A religious group with unusual beliefs and a controlling leader.

economy—The system by which money and goods flow through society.

hijack—To seize control of a vehicle by force.

impeach—To bring formal charges of misconduct against an elected leader; if found guilty of those charges, the leader is removed from office.

Islam—One of the world's largest religions; it is based on the teachings of the prophet Muhammad.

nuclear—Relating to energy that comes from the splitting or merging of atoms.

overdose—Too much of a drug taken at once.

radiation—Invisible but harmful rays and particles given off by nuclear materials.

scandal—A disgraceful incident that draws public attention.

sentiment—A view or attitude based on strong emotions.

suicide—The act of taking one's own life.

superpower—A powerful country that leads other countries.

FURTHER READING

Anderson, Dale. *Watergate: Scandal in the White House*. Mankato, Minn.: Compass Point Books, 2006.

Bobek, Milan, ed. *Decades of the Twentieth Century: the 1970s*. Pittsburgh: Eldorado Ink, 2005.

Feigenbaum, Aaron. *Emergency at Three Mile Island*. New York: Bearport Publishing, 2007.

Kappes, Serena. *Hank Aaron*. Minneapolis, Minn.: Lerner Publications, 2005.

Marcovitz, Hal. *The Vietnam War*. Farmington Hills, Mich.: Lucent Books, 2007.

Ochester, Betsy. *Richard M. Nixon: America's 37th President*. Danbury, Conn.: Children's Press, 2005.

Poole, Rebecca. *Jimi Hendrix*. Minneapolis, Minn.: Lerner Publications, 2006.

Rosinsky, Natalie M. *The Kent State Shootings*. Mankato, Minn.: Compass Point Books, 2008.

Sonneborn, Liz. *Murder at the 1972 Olympics in Munich*. New York: Rosen Publishing, 2002.

Van Meter, Larry A. *United States v. Nixon: The Question of Executive Privilege*. New York: Chelsea House, 2007.

Wagner, Heather Lehr. *Anwar Sadat and Menachem Begin*. New York: Chelsea House Publishers, 2007.

Wahab, Shaista and Barry Youngerman. *A Brief History of Afghanistan*. New York: Facts on File, 2007.

Wiest, Andrew. *The Vietnam War*. New York: Rosen, 2008.

INTERNET RESOURCES

<http://www.baseballhalloffame.org/hofers/detail.jsp?playerId=110001>
View pictures and video of home-run hitter Hank Aaron. The National
Baseball Hall of Fame & Museum offers this tribute to the slugger.

<http://www.washingtonpost.com/wp-srv/politics/special/watergate/>
From the Washington Post, this special report provides fascinating details on
the Watergate scandal. It includes a timeline of key events.

<http://www.jimmycarterlibrary.org/documents/hostages.phtml>
Read more about the Iran hostage crisis in this site by the Jimmy Carter
Library and Museum. It includes a diary kept by one of the hostages.

INDEX

PICTURE CREDITS

Illustration credits: AP/Wide World Photos: 1 (top), 9 (bottom), 10, 15, 23 (top), 24, 25 (top), 31, 44, 45 (bottom), 51 (top); Courtesy Jimmy Carter Library: 42, 43; Courtesy Gerald R. Ford Library: 33, 37 (top); Getty Images: 1 (left, top right), 4, 5, 20, 22, 50 (top); AFP/Getty Images: 12, 52, 55; Focus On Sport/Getty Images: 25 (bottom); Michael Ochs Archives/Getty Images: 20, 21 (top); Popperfoto/Getty Images: 9 (top), 16; Time & Life Pictures/Getty Images: 17, 21 (bottom), 29 (bottom), 49 (bottom); Roger Viollet/Getty Images: 27 (top); Ron Ilan/© The State of Israel: 29 (top); Sa'ar Ya'acov/© The State of Israel: 13, 23 (bottom), 40, 41; Lucasfilm/20th Century Fox/The Kobal Collection: 35 (bottom); Paramount/The Kobal Collection: 34, 38, 39 (top); Universal/The Kobal Collection: 35 (top); Dennis Brack/Landov: 39 (bottom); dpa/Landov: 54; Library of Congress: 6, 32, 45 (top); NASA Johnson Space Center: 18; National Archives and Records Administration: 19, 26, 47; Courtesy Richard Nixon Presidential Library and Museum: 1 (bottom right), 7, 8, 30; Photofest: 48; Courtesy Ronald Reagan Library and Museum: 57; B.H. Moody/Saudi Aramco World/SAWDIA: 28; used under license from Shutterstock, Inc.: 14, 27 (bottom), 36, 37 (bottom), 46, 49 (top); U.S. Department of Defense: 50 (bottom), 51 (bottom), 53.

Cover photos: Getty Images (Earth Day 1970; Vietnam soldier); courtesy Richard Nixon Presidential Library and Museum (Nixon leaves the White House).